THE NATIONAL POETRY SERIES

The National Poetry Series was established in 1978 to ensure the publication of five collections of poetry annually through five participating publishers. The Series is funded annually by Amazon Literary Partnership, the Gettinger Family Foundation, Bruce Gibney, HarperCollins Publishers, The Stephen and Tabitha King Foundation, Lannan Foundation, Newman's Own Foundation, Anna and Olafur Olafsson, Penguin Random House, the Poetry Foundation, Elise and Steven Trulaske, and the National Poetry Series Board of Directors.

2019 COMPETITION WINNERS

Field Music by Alexandria Hall
Chosen by Rosanna Warren for Ecco

Little Big Bully by Heid E. Erdrich
Chosen by Amy Gerstler for Penguin Books

Fractal Shores by Diane Louie
Chosen by Sherod Santos for University of Georgia Press

Thrown in the Throat by Benjamin Garcia
Chosen by Kazim Ali for Milkweed Editions

An Incomplete List of Names by Michael Torres
Chosen by Raquel Salas Rivera for Beacon Press

LITTLE
BIG
BULLY

HEID E. ERDRICH

PENGUIN BOOKS

PENGUIN BOOKS

An imprint of Penguin Random House LLC

penguinrandomhouse.com

LIBRARY OF CONGRESS CATALOGING-IN-PUBLICATION DATA

Names: Erdrich, Heid E. (Heid Ellen) author.
Title: Little big bully / Heid E. Erdrich.
Description: First. | [New York] : Penguin Books, [2020] | Series: National
poetry series
Identifiers: LCCN 2020005406 (print) | LCCN 2020005407 (ebook) | ISBN
9780143135920 (paperback) | ISBN 9780525507512 (ebook)
Subjects: LCGFT: Poetry.
Classification: LCC PS3555.R418 L58 2020 (print) | LCC PS3555.R418
(ebook) | DDC 811/.54—dc23
LC record available at https://lccn.loc.gov/2020005406
LC ebook record available at https://lccn.loc.gov/2020005407

Printed in the United States of America
10 9 8 7 6 5 4 3 2 1

Set in Garamond 3 LT Pro
Designed by Beth Tondreau

INDAANIS, INGOZIS
&
NINAABEM

For Eliza, who survived the polar vortex with me.

For the girl who melted an ice giant before it could eat us all.

For we must all swallow hope to burn the fear within us.

ACKNOWLEDGMENTS

My gratitude to editors who chose some of the poems in this collection, often in earlier versions, to include in the following publications: *Poetry*, *American Indian Culture and Research Journal*, *Kenyon Review*, *Contra Viento*, *Still Point Press*, *Zocalo Public Square*, *Water~Stone Review*, *The Arkansas International*, *Literary Hub*, *The Rumpus*, *Truth to Power* anthology from *Cutthroat Journal*, and *Mud City Journal*.

For support of my work and for space and time to write, my thanks to the Native Arts and Cultures Foundation, Lannan Foundation, Northwestern University Center for Native American and Indigenous Studies, Hedgebrook, University of Minnesota, Morris, and the Vermont Studio Center.

Abiding thanks to Amy Gerstler for picking *Little Big Bully* for the National Poetry Series and for affording me one of the most gratifying moments of my life. Thanks to Beth Dial and the National Poetry Series and its funders. My thanks to Paul Slovak and Penguin for all they have done to bring this and other poetry books to the world.

Many people were there for me these past few years and these are just a few I thank: Angie Erdrich, Jim Denomie, Todd Bockley, Jonathan Thunder, and Kate Kysar. I am deeply grateful to my sister writers, my company on the road: LeAnne Howe, Deborah Miranda, Janet McAdams, Natalie Diaz, Jennifer Foerster, and the Hedgebrook gathering of Laura Da', Sara Marie Ortiz, Cassandra Lopez, Terese Mailhot, and DeLanna Studi. My thanks to my fellow scholars at The Native American Literature Symposium, to Kelly Wisecup and Mark Turcotte, and to my colleagues and students at Augsburg University low-residency MFA. Thanks as well to the poets of *New Poets of Native Nations*. To Molly McGlennen, Stacy Pratt, Ryan Rhadigan, Tiffany Midge, and Sheila Regan, thanks for reviews and interviews and the clarity they bring to me and other writers.

For important conversations that lent me clarity, my thanks and love to Eric Gansworth and Rosy Simas. To Louise, your generosity of spirit, your bravery and sisterhood made much of this work possible, miigwech! Kismet and Pallas, in a roaring world your voices are the sweet, still spot I need and I thank you. I am deeply grateful to Andrea Carlson for the art on the cover of this book, and for talking all day and night and all the next morning so I could see I had built the backbone of this book and it would stand.

John Burke, you charge my words and power my work, always.

Miigwech!

CONTENTS

LITTLE BIG BULLY

How

Loves How I love you How you How we hang on words How eaten with need How we need to eat How weevils sift the wheat How cold it is How thick with hoarfrost ice slick sleet freeze How wintry the mix How full of angst How gut sick How blue lipped How we drink How we drink a health How we care How easy over as eggs How it all slides How absurd How yet tender we all How wrapped in a thick coat How battered How slender the flesh How we wrap ourselves How many selves we all How I miss you many How I see you How your eyes warm mine How tiny am I inside How enormous my need How you open an old-fashioned satchel How deep it yawns How bleak this need How like winter How it yet catches the light How brilliant the sun dogs parhelion moon dogs paraselene phenomenon optic How fetching your spectacles How my thumbs might fit alongside the slope of your nose How my own glasses slide down my thin bridge How ridiculous the theory of the bridge How inane the bibble babble How we grew to be friends How we grew thumbs How opposable we all How we grew sparks How we blew up a fire How angry How incensed How we resist How we bead up drops How water will not run How we distract How loud the dog snores How loudly How noisy the snow grows How many degrees below How we fret How again How we all came here How did we come How did we How loves How did we come to this

✹

✹✹

✹✹✹

✹✹✹✹

✹✹✹✹✹

✹✹✹✹✹✹

✹✹✹✹✹✹✹

✹✹✹✹✹✹✹✹

✹ ✹✹✹✹✹✹ ✹✹

✹✹✹✹✹✹✹✹ ✹✹

✹✹✹ ✹✹✹ ✹✹✹✹

Sovereign Love

When I look upon the beloved   the real beloved   not the beloved of memoirs
made up in revenge   but   the active generator of love   the love maker
When I   when   When I look upon you
Beloved   I might avert my gaze   let it stray only to your hands
then up to your throat
        It is only in holding your eyes away from mine
        that I can stay sovereign in my love
It is only for you   not from you   It is more than state or nation
This love is itself unto itself   The only name it needs it speaks within me
Call it what you will   It will answer

Variations True

Subtle color variations of lilac
keep coming back to me   late 1970's
I asked my adult cousins   in Germany
What did you do in The War?
We were young   they said   we didn't know
All was normal   they said   *normal*   auf Deutsch
We took our bikes   they said   out of the *Stadt*   the city
They went to gather flowers   some seasonal fest they biked to   to dance to eat to sing
I imagine them in wide skirts—with aprons maybe—on curvy bikes with wire baskets
filled with lilac blossoms overflowing and abundant and all the young things
I imagine them pedaling back on a day that happens later but time collapses
in these instances and I see them braking heavily when they find the city ruined
then they run to the river—that actually happened—survive waves of flame
too late for my father's grandparents already dead in the rubble   buried in debris
the city later piled into an enormous hill that grew over green and inviting along
the same paths my cousins biked and recalled when I asked   *What did you do?*
Normal   they said   I never understood instead kept lilacs in my head
So many pinks and faded inky purples that turn blue in age so many stages of one bloom
that might not grow there but my mind maybe stood *lilac* as substitute for a German word
Normal   they said   I never knew how many variations of a vision we can spin
to make one image that might not even have been true but now is now and now I know we do

All Nations

I would like to think they've gone off somewhere safer
    chevron finch wing   split swallow tail
                Not gone gone   just off   not halved
    clap of doves   yellowhammer flicker

Even now *extinction* sounds a bit   what? otherworldly   dinos on lost islands
    meadowlark vibrato   loon tremolo   warbler warble
warblers once a thousand specks too quick to see except as a totality
            a trembling tree
Some think it our accomplishment   say *extermination*

Blackbirds contract   like a thought cloud above a cartoon   one notion
suddenly turns a helix   a message   one nation

Like to think they've gone off   *it's these floods drove them away*
    the way fear makes me think I'll fly apart
    leave my shoes on earth

    So I weigh my body down   a grounded creature
Like to think   of the badger   I honk to avoid tragedy   bad enough
two lanes make a monarch murderer of me
To think how aerodynamics save most   boosted over my windshield
    the badger no doubt drawn to the road to eat killed
dragonflies checkers skippers grasshoppers moths   my tiny extermination

Before I weighed my body down   I was so small so sure   butterflies loved me
trusted my outstretched hands   painted ladies landed
    licked salt off my palms
    then the corners of my mouth

Native child of the last postwar   I heard *extermination*   in the policy called *Termination*
saw yellow stars and children packed like cattle   their faces   our future faces
And even when I knew our grandfather fought to stop   their termination of our tribe
and even when robins kept spring from silence   when eagles started their return
                              my fear flew off with me   I knew   won't unknow
whole nations can be unmade   on paper   and in cages

They did it once they'll try again

                              I would like   someone to set it down
We are as made
wild   original   to say it on paper   *We are the children of creation*
                                  under some protection   our rights equal eagle's

They would like to think we've gone
Not gone gone   off   not halved

Extinction sounds like other worlds   other words   *extermination*   *Termination*

Wild sparrows glean my yard   scrape up what's left
                                then they'll be gone off
I like to think
        they will be back
                              We try
to make a stop for birds   a home for beasts   a possum once
                                  a woodchuck mom
who sunbathed on our deck chair   nursed her pups   before
                                the neighbor's dachshunds
                                found them out
The fence declines

the wild beasts retreat
like a child

my mistake   I like to think   how
to think   we are safe somehow
                        behind fences
safe on the road's shoulder
                                    safe somewhere on paper
or that we   or any nation
could go off somewhere   safer
that there's somewhere   still out there
closer to wild

Fauxskins

Their war paint and stoic pout we laugh at   we can't help it
Their profile pictures   DNA reveals   their family secrets

When she was dying   *our grandmother told me*   *how ashamed she was to be . . .*
Pappy would get drunk   *and say*   *"You're an Injun and you'll always be . . ."*
My great-grandmother   *the full-blooded* (Generokee)   *didn't need papers to be . . .*

Their *high cheekbones*   Their *dark-haired* aunts   Their uncle's *nickel profile*
                It's all phrenology to them

I've always been so close to nature so close to animals so close to rocks   so close to you   I am right
behind you getting better than you at the language the beadwork the smudge
the water protection and skirt shaming and de-colonizing and outrage and being . . .

so spiritual   so yes very   spiritual your   *spirit animal*

Red Pony   High Wolf   Sky Wolf   Flying Wolf   Woof Woof
        Names always in English   (ancestors spirits speak English
                                apparently)

Tell you what   fill their ancestors' skulls with beans
or dig them up some place like Wounded Knee   You get my drift?
It's too easy   for them to be . . .

How small and mean that makes me   *Why you wannabe so mean?*
What does it matter when   Geronimo (Sitting Bull) (Crazy Horse)
                      . . . came to me in a dream

It's never women in those dreams   Never a message to vote in tribal elections

or get that GED   or go for a run or party party party
                         Who says the ancestors weren't fun?

Why do they only work their ways in one-time visions?   They stay in us   every day

I'm part Indian   Which part?   *I'm probably more Indian than you*
When?   Where do you feel it?   *In my heart I've always been NDN*

Do you feel it in your
                    health disparities wealth disparities educational gaps
                    in your risk factors your suicides your youth at risk
                    your couch surfer your addicted your sterilized
                    your missing and murdered your sisters your girls
                    your dead cousin dead uncles   your people?

It skipped a generation to me   *I'm a throwback*   *No one talks about it*
                                                      No one else in my family wants to be . . .

Fauxskins   blood seekers   shifters   creepy the way they want in
                                                      they want *in* us—*inside* us
                                                      want to dress in our dead
                                                      to wear our past and skins
                                                      dispossess us again
                                                                          take what's left
                                                      of what it means to be we—our plurality

Smallness   meanness   Now I'm the colonizer—me!

How can it hurt to let them in   re-indigenize   swell the tribe?
Isn't that the prophecy?   *A nation is coming*   *The seventh gen*
that fire where we will all be returned to the way things used to be

So were they always there with us?   Did we always hang crystal dreamcatchers
                                       Should we make room for a yurt by our tipi?
Or room on the shelf?   The list of Native Authors of Indigenous Descent
the publishers crowing   the university of diversity   the museum the funder
Should we leave them under the impression?   Failing to understand complexity
                                                        tribal sovereignty

                    We decide who is we

There are so many we   570-some tribes that other tribes and laws agree
Oh   laws!   There goes old colonizer me!

You know she's not really   *You know she used to say she's . . .*
                                Now they're all . . . you know . . .   Metis

You know   there but for the
                          quantum rules   tribal rolls
                          per cap   casinos   allotments
                          fur trade journals   conversions   census
                                       bad math   blood math
                                                        ancestry
                              (dis)enrollment

                                       (go I)
                                              goes me

Story of These Creatures

Three creatures in a story
            I could pick them randomly
a girl a   woods a beast

The spruce out my window
sheds patches of bark   worried
by some bird who bares the trunk

She's back at it busy
her bullying leaves my spruce   exposed
red core in patches
her tail a bold kickstand
black and white as type

Three-toed woodpecker   tender
of spruce   her only food
beetles beneath cold bark   dormant

Three creatures in a story cycle
I never blame the bird
the tree the   beetles
        the story's up to me
might as well type it
        black and bold

How old?   8 or   9 or   10   worried when boys
        plain boys   who fished
rode bikes with me   same as me
                but white
in jeans and hooded jackets   transform   exposed as beasts
        like in a storybook forest

me a maid alone   or a girl saint
forced on the road   *forced to marry*
like church book stories

Say nothing   says some part in me
        some bully some   tender of my temperature
    froze me
pinned me like their pocket knives

How long?   (it had been hidden)   dormant knowledge
    (this would happen)
How long?   (did I forget where)
I first heard the word   *rape*
    snickered   like a fun idea

No   *that* did not happen   nothing happened   if asked   *nothing happened*
roughed up against a tree
spruce tree that hid what they did   I hid what   they did   nothing

These creatures in a story cycle
I never blame the tree the fish   the bikes   the stories told
    are genius really
    little bullies   scripted so early
    they make   one big bully decree
    treaty between me and me
    that ceded me from me
    reserved the little me for me

Not

Not the girl in the rambler staring out her window every summer—not allowed out
Not the girl whose dad left his pistol under the pillow where we jumped on the bed
Not the girl who wore only undershirts at home on her daddy's lap
Not the girl who cleaned-dressed-bathed fed her little sisters dogfood if she had to
Not the girl who could not read who married the odd jobs man
Not the girl who parked with her dad on country roads then by bars—her mom stayed home
Not the girl who thrilled at the drop off kiss from the dad whose kids she babysat
Not the girl who got a car got a puppy got a trip when she gave her baby away
Not the girl whose cousin hit her with his rifle until she knelt and did it
Not the girl who never looked at me again who never talked to me again who never laughed
Not the girl who swore me not to tell who told me I would die who ran off and married
Not the girl another girl and then another girl then so many many girls while I was still a girl
Not the girl but a woman who was not has not did not would not could not will not not not

Story of the Charismenace

Once upon a time a woman

found a wee thing out in the wide world   on a rock or cliff or plain
or it called to her in her garden
                                        All versions are true

She found it in a heap   messy and flopped   a whelp   really
                yet magnetic

                                        Drawn as women are
(woman—young one—need)   she did as women do

It grew fast   cried-laughed-howled   in feral madness in meanness
built a cage and trapped its own madness in   then wore the cage
                        it made a fashion statement   it had a certain charm
                                        badass and mad   madass

She threw her tameness to its charisma   but
                        Wild -v- Tame   a bad match

She read in this something like   Indigenous
something like   colonized
                        but still

(though by now it grew huge as weather   a menace who
                raged and shamed and raged and shamed
                        crumpled all who loved)

                        she didn't judge   wild being what it is to this world

The woman said nothing   The woman said nothing   The woman said nothing

When nothing is said   the story gets starved   in that way she said

                    the end

Killed Darling

Raw fur and teeth—a teratoma of a beast
breast-kept and unkempt
baptized before born then
sent to be reborn
it gets a better form this time
rabbit blind and bottle fed
not much hope it will grow
and yet it blinks open
        eyes all brown and wild

Territory Was Not Virgin and Neither Was I (Virgin)

Born overflowing all giving   you never could take
what we never gave   what I held back
sky fat with rain   water dropping my name slowly on my lips

no part of me you could remove from this water
she touches everything
never alone so even
what you broke   blew up   bomb of droplets   collective
thunder sounding   sounding   resounding

no wonder you grew afraid
my voice refused you   all of you
erased even the names faces places they tried to take us
so only a steady music stays   the urgency of rain

neither could you take it with your cannon that turns sound against bodies
profound vibration shot through bone
          shock to the ears the brain the dreams
or water cannons   water usurped turned to weapon
          turned to ice turned to burn

they waded away with water   took water back
dispersed the hurt across the globe
the globe of water the only territory the only country the only kinship
          the one we would not give

if we give ourselves to anything   we give ourselves to water
if I give myself to anything   I give myself to water
not bride or prize or slave   but daughter then grown woman then wave

next to wave next to wave   no more yours than rain
         rain dropping slowly   so even you could hear it
                                    knows you
                                    knows your name

Face to Face

How can you stop
touching your face
when I can barely resist
touching your face?
    It's the septum I crave
    and now
            but for now
our quarantine is Joker
taunting Batman
It's right under your nose!
    We've seen nothing like this
all these long days between us
every question unanswered
makes me want to coax the words
         stroke your
(I look it up)   *philtrum*
            love charm
    Oh I can withhold
my touch retreats from
your eminence your arch
your cheek plane chin orbit
brow ridge temples   your notch
your fossa   basin of tears
your lobe your canal
           No these
do not so much tempt me
but that slope and dip
tenderest of ports my pinkie fits
where spirit pushed a fingertip
into the clay of us   hushed us
with a touch so we could not tell

all we saw and must forget
in order to be born
in order to shine the way
        your eyes
        oh oh   stop it with your eyes!
Your eyes just lead me to your smile
then above to that cupid's bow
I wish and wish I could plant a kiss
draw all that forgotten knowledge out
but so many touches undone
murdered between want
and what we must
           we must
   We close our eyes in two beds
   too much risk to sleep foot
   to head and breathe our dreams
   into the one thing we once were
           truly not knowing
           we will ever be again

North of Love

A blank lake covered in snow
whatever we do there will be writ
printed white on white
shadowed blue then blown to hints
of what went on in the terrible wonder of cold
in this our north of love

Oh   we know   you want us to shut up about it
but we will go on saying love is   or love does   or love will

If we can   we tell it in Ojibwe
where love does love with you and who you love
                                    reflexive love

Oh   we know you are watching us   You read us
In the north we've so long been prey
we feel eyes sly and green-gold   on us always
                                beware any feeble movement or distraction
You do nothing but distract

Still even this year
ice monoliths erupt
and we risk our lips to melt
next to art   cold art
already going back to lake as water
water taking water up and out then back
in some reflexive state the north can teach us

We know
you see us we see you we know you fear us we fear you we know you beat us we will beat you

Oh   we hear you laughing—your cruelty   yap-yap yap-yap   yaps

It is not that love alone will do this for us   we know
no engine of abstraction matters
unless it drives us north of love

BearAncestry.com

Do not mistake me for an Ojibwe teller of tradition teller of the living lit of long-dead tellers but do count me as a teller of still-alive stories It is true that humans become bears mostly harmless Once they honeyed love upon us broke the hive and plundered Once they hugged like bears and were bears literal bears with shitty tails reeking lumbering gutting garbage cans then slumber came which figuratively means the weaker one fell for love   dumb move and done before weaker ones and many fell off earth out of orbit lost as Bowie's midnight blue wails

Bears care most for their hungers which means we get in the way collateral damage of beastly rampage which now makes me think these alive stories do not speak of bears but something human and more beastly political and public We started with love foolish love which should have worried us Love is how any beast would read our weakness When the beast reads us we can feel a psychic scan bright on our skin and that smell you know that one the smell when your

> lips numb
> the smell
> you taste

✳

✳ ✳

✳ ✳ ✳

✳ ✳ ✳ ✳

✳ ✳ ✳ ✳ ✳

✳ ✳ ✳ ✳ ✳ ✳

✳ ✳ ✳ ✳ ✳ ✳ ✳

✳ ✳ ✳ ✳ ✳ ✳ ✳ ✳

✳ ✳ ✳ ✳ ✳ ✳ ✳ ✳ ✳

✳ ✳ ✳ ✳ ✳ ✳ ✳ ✳ ✳ ✳

✳ ✳ ✳ ✳ ✳ ✳ ✳ ✳ ✳ ✳ ✳

✳ ✳ ✳ ✳ ✳ ✳ ✳ ✳ ✳ ✳ ✳

✳ ✳ ✳ ✳ ✳ ✳ ✳ ✳ ✳ ✳

✳ ✳ ✳ ✳ ✳ ✳ ✳ ✳ ✳

✳ ✳ ✳ ✳ ✳ ✳ ✳ ✳

✳ ✳ ✳ ✳ ✳ ✳ ✳

✳ ✳ ✳ ✳ ✳ ✳

✳ ✳ ✳ ✳ ✳

✳ ✳ ✳ ✳

✳ ✳ ✳

✳ ✳

✳

Melania Won't Leave You (though she retires to her private island Melanesia where she learns the Tongan word *tabu*)

She wants to be set apart   she wants to be alone   though
she will not stop talking to you   she sounds like mink secrets
her eyes plead pools   her dark eyes lined   lead lined to survive
she groans a human groan and yet   you hate her   hate her   hate her
        Get on this train it keeps on going   hate hate hate hate   hate
This is not your nature   someone dragged you here   some bully who
makes us seethe   make us wish the bully dead
      then their work is done
      but still this train roars on
Next stop   anyone who loved him   anyone who would not leave him
The one who will not stop talking   with her deeply leaden fur-lashed eyes
She begins a tale   something shimmering and wise   but broken so unknowable
She says again   all she ever wanted was to be unhunted   you hounds
She says   you unhumans   you *inhumans*
She says it lower   over and over   rougher   until she grrrs until   just sound
a mean sound you know   you know means   you

Big Sir

massive block of a man takes the light turns up his chin

                           sun exists to shine for him

    the deep shadow of his form

    forms a field   a force   repulsion and pull

    of someone brutal and strong

               cold eclipse   his proximity   shivers in heat

something back   from childhood

when we learned   in the taste of grit and dirt   to get up

            be safe or brave

learned two sides   the line   hide behind   or step up

    but never get between

          the mean mass

          and his light

          he needs

          his shine

needs that dark too   the one made for design   that blacker than black

that deep shade

      trailing shadow of mad dad bad boy stalker wife-beater boss

we all hide   where we grew   comfortable in what we knew

    where to stand off to his bad side

    or we let him stand between us   and them

               us or them!

               us or them!

       behemoth shadow so terrible

his need so big   we just get smaller without melting

        he keeps us cool

such shade here   such screen against   too bright right
                                                        or dazzle of wrong
                    righter right to wash the wrong

darker than that design dark his shadow   a cape
                                                 no one tugs
                                                 we just ski along
his tow an excuse not to choose
until he needs to hear like the jesus   some believe
                                          craves praise
                                          even a lame note
behind you   (sometimes stepping)   *on your strong*
big strong   (something wrong to even we)   *we so*
small please we need please you big Sir we please Sir   on our knees

Dear Demeter—Dear Earth (where Hades is the noncustodial parent)

First   in the dark world of a crying child
he will think you ruined his offspring

He'll say "milk spoilt" and "mama's boy"

Soon enough   he will hate you and hold hostage
all the love he can wring from
a small   terrified   being

Then   when the shining child smiles
and the damned underworld is seen
dank and relentless   for what it is
he will see that you invented fire

He will see you kindled   with your body
an illuminated being   a soul devoted
a bright likeness of the father

He will love you   He will bless you

He will try to   make you   His

Degree

Who bellowed *I'll teach you a lesson!*   not my parents
Whose mom was it called me *Egg Head*   called our dad *The Professor*
Who smacked with their hand's back   *When will you ever learn?*
Who knocked me   *Book Smart—no common sense*
Which grown men shoulder slapped me so   I jolted   stumbled   stuttered
Whose dad kicked me in the backside   *Damn hippie Indian freak!*
Whose dad was it called his belt *The Educator*   why remember?
Whose education did I earn?   Oh   I learned
        to a lesser degree

Perpetual Communion of Jr. High

She used a brittle gloss of sugar
as emblem of her girlhood game
the kind of translucent candies
watermelon green apple cinnamon hot
      Eyes closed
you heard the crinkle and unwrap
as you stood   tongue out
If you were in   it went in
If you were out   you spit out
the twist of cellophane or swallowed at
The Jock Priestess of Jr. High's command
Or maybe you carried your own candies
showed her your tongue stained pink
      or green or red
           stuck it out hard and passed
True her goons kicked you in the ass
but to this day any artificial taste
takes you back   There was a time
you stood apart   from all of that

Untaught

Untaught the way the body switches like a road in the mountains
Untaught my own permission my yes and my no
Untaught the dimensions of loss   the rubber bubble of it   expanding from the moment
Untaught the dwindling of enormity until it fit in me   actually in me   then grew out
Untaught the way to catch myself when falling into feeling
Untaught to swim the reedy slough of hurt   or lust or hunger   or hopelessness
Untaught   untutored   unimproved   the baby of the universe   egg   oh so new
Untaught my own math   my reduction my dozens my thousands   my lessons to unlearn

Bond Shock

The base of you   perhaps the bookish you   allowed how
their loudness went before you   like a torch
that touched you too   too hot   but cleared a path
A pathetic need that   a need they would use   Later on
            on rug-burned knees   you knew   you saw
the paper edges of you curl   ash taste
singed origin of a bitter mouth   a deep sore
so sorry so   so sorry

Circumstance

Three hundred thousand years ago
creatures alike as dog and wolf and coyote diverged
      unknown circumstances   paths split   that was it
                        or so I read

      Then I walked   took a random way   by pastel chalk on sidewalks
          Passiontide   *Passover*   or *Easter*

      to sit me down at last to read again

The wood floors creak at his feet   announce I am found
He is vain   so his ironic socks   identify him
                    against the scuffed floorboards
                         of this dim coffeeshop

My hand strays to my cup   I look up
he orders more without asking me   he pays

    I must have left   my tracks   maybe at the college
                      where I stopped to watch
        a young woman who
        hair raining across her red face
        traced a pastel mermaid's tail as banner   *Earth Day*
        or circumstance walked me
        into the wrong café

I picked the wrong table   or I always pick the wrong table or
read the wrong way

          Coydog   wyote   coywolf
he gulps and stares sideways

          I'm no prey   he thinks I'm game

Three hundred thousand years ago wolf
we were   and coyote   we diverged

our paths split and that should have been it
but now he sidles closer whines
                              Your hair's different   What you do to it?

My hair   my wild streak
my feral brown fall   aged with fire
                    my only me I wish seen
                                   I've never done a thing with my hair

but let it speak for me   move in attitudes
my braid flipping   shoulder side or over a breast
a curtain   now a convenience   when I try to skirt his eyes

Just past an eclipse   so he's dragging   crazy talking about
how he kept up   all night   breaking it off with Moon
                                        how she ran raw faced and hid her eyes

Doesn't skip a beat from love of her
to bait for me   *We two should get together soon*

Circumstance   vanity   chance
                    Spring trembles like a pastel thing

I catch him this time   when he leans
                    grasp his chin hairs and say it plain

                    Rage owns a shadow named shame
                    my husband keeps my bed
                    the moon may have bled
                    I slept

Little Big

Like the raw woman at the dog pound whose shoulders say she's done with some drug or someone
She's still young but this is not about love She tunes her ears to vicious snarls says *Yes that one* The
workers say *No we don't think so* but she insists on that body of fury that vibration of animal urge to
hurt to bite and bite the hand to feed up some of what it learned   to serve it back in snaps
because she sees in him a wounded pup the velvet ball of pug   what the dog once was
She coos low ungloves tucks him under her arm She knows she can   knows this one knows

                                     what it is to be
                                     used like a gun

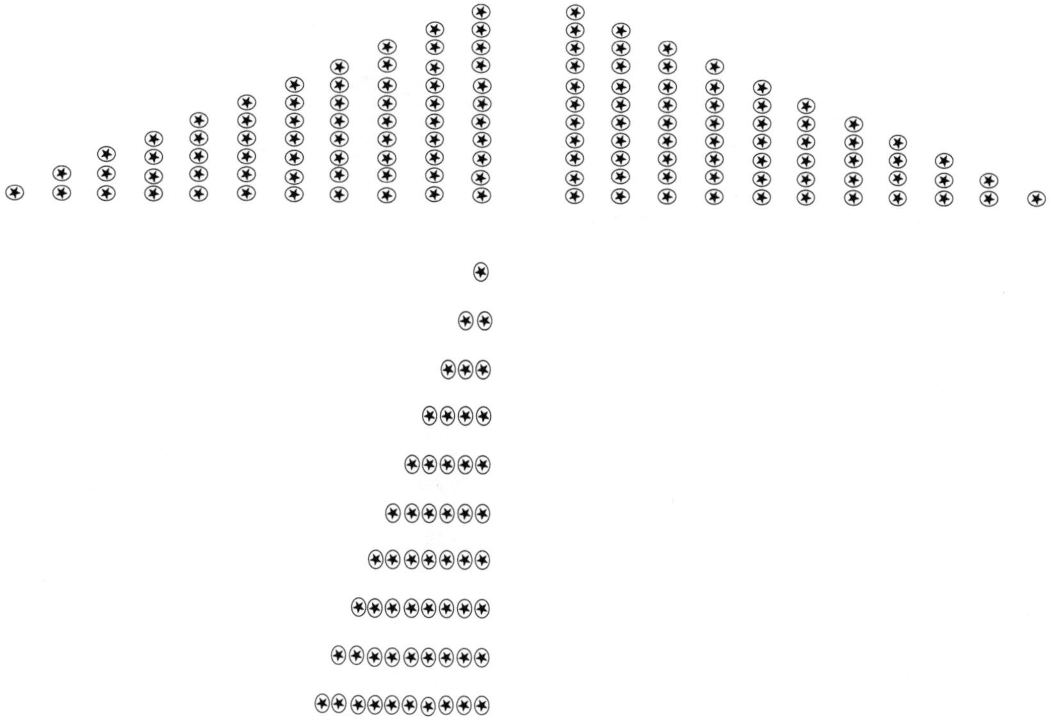

Always the First Time

I saw the second plane hit real time then the towers fell and neighbors grouped outside weeping so I went to the dry-eyed one then we stood in front of her tv until I told her I had outpatient surgery and my sister said *you take care of you* which is all we can do and I did enter that bleak waiting room where the towers continued their fall on loop and everyone on camera looked up about to duck unlike the few women waiting there who did not lift their eyes to the screens but spoke into cell phones urgently and none in English so I cannot know or guess what all of it meant or what it even meant to me to see rage vented on a scale that tried to match damage done in other lands kept so far away until that day that morning when I opened my legs to let the surgeon do what we agreed would keep me alive if not fertile alive unlike so many of his clients mostly not interested in fertility he said *mostly prostitutes* he said as my knees jerked away from his head because no man should say that when well no doctor should and then he asked who I thought hijacked the planes and I said *Al-Qaeda* and he said how could I know and who was Al-Qaeda anyhow and I thought he should know but what I said was *we will all know soon* and he went on with his bloody burning work while I tried with all my might not to think of that first hurt endured tried not to loop that first time when it is always the first time every time every threat always the same time any time someone enters in rage in revenge against all my kind

Put Down

Kneel or crouch or stoop
low   go low   be humble

in the face of danger or random rage

Have a life   if you must   but hidden
from the creature gaze
the saurian raptor intelligence

that finds you   virtually   in days

Kneel or crouch or stoop—
pick a clean place   they say

rock or tree root
where you ask help
not for yourself

Avert your eyes
not so you do not see
but so you are not seen

You go so low   go under
sub radar   go to the ground
go dark radio silent

             Shiver in it   the power of it
     what he controls he owns

     whoever he keeps down
          gets him up   keeps them low

Kneel or crouch or stoop—
pick a clean place   they say

rock or tree root
where you ask help

not for yourself

Public Grief

This is not my grief
but a small hole lightless
penetrating the globe of family
so now all stands still
ringed by light snow
ringed by bright lights

This is not my grief
but a lightless hole through the human globe
surrounded by cameras yammering
brilliant stills and stunned silence grown   so loud
it weighs down the flowers

daisies   carnations   lilies   mums
all the flowers ever
left in memorial along with
all the letters and petitions
and again the promise of never

This is not my grief
but a small hole   lightless
penetrating the light show
the weight of all-the-ever flowers
cameras and microphones
speechless   unspeakable   there are no words
but words and words and words

This is not my grief
but a black and white vortex   a crush
that collapses   sucks in   swallows whole

This is not my grief   but

                                    a terrible   a particular

a small hole   deep beyond belief
deeper   deep enough
                                    to own its depth
                                    to be depth alone

Nothing to Forget

Glitter and smoke   blue lights
a wreck we wish we never met

Glitter and smoke or a firehose
Blue lights and a slow line

Gauntlet through debris and emergency vans
slow going   troopers who motion
so we roll the window down

nothing to see here   move along

No   nothing at all between us and the road
nothing under the roll of white sheeting   spread to hide

spread shoulder to hillside   cops popping under   then out to yell

                         last place you want to be today
Last place someone was today

cop cars blocking lanes
forgetting they've forced us to stall

                         nothing to see here   move along

Last thing we want to see today

That post   we do not look
That text   we do not read

Need to know   That's how we've cordoned off
terror and your threat   until it's something we forget   your wreck

The Pacifist Grows Mean

Courage   when it speaks
might be a small peaceful man
gray-haired   of no color   unrighteous
                  but right

You would be as kind   but no
inside every handshake is a fist
your deep-born peace also knows this

Your peace grows gravel-voiced   erodes
grains of sand in wind   two centuries
of scouring abrasion   day to day to day

At first it hurts   like a voice leaving us
or the opposite   a stillness taken over
hundreds of years of whispers in one roar

Your peace defeats itself
called to defend   your peace finds a line
then finds any line takes sides

One day your blood jumps up
one day your warrior blood jeers
you speak your piece

You boo   and hiss and rant
you spend years drowning out
that sound without sound   your peace

You damp it down   cache it deep
that largeness of humanity—
that quiet that once held you

Before you were claimed by your chorus
before your peace worked for others
before you grew to know   what it might mean
                                   to be so mean

Zeno's Indians

```
***********
**********
*********
********
*******
******
*****
****
***
**
*
```

There is only one Indian* There is no Native American** There are Native Americans*** This one rez-raised (in the minority****) might like to be more real than that one urban-rez-raised (coming majority) and still that one adopted-out and back in with stories to tell as real as that one learned at university   learned how to tell the real old-time indin' tales in their original language and this one (provided with millions of dollars in social programs*****) shrugging off success like that's not power enough and that one giving a perm in an old gas-station remodeled for the beauty parlor she always dreamed on the two-lane blacktop a hundred miles from her reservation in the next town over and that one holding the door for an elder (he calls her Grandma******) and driving her around weekends and helping her to bed who knows his relatives and avoids them and this one blazing the country—Turtle Island—with empowerment and edutainment and good-hearted as the day is an exhausting blur of anger and youth to love and this one   Well you get the point the pointlessness or pointedness   The One Indian is 128/128ths CIB******* and would not be recognized as Indian by the Federal government******** The One Indian's descendants will marry and have children for seven generations before federal recognition of one whole Indian will be possible********* (or once for tribal recognition if love came through the right tribe **********) Zeno had a (commodity***********) cheese and (must have been a Minnesotan ************) because every time he cut the cheese in half   his guest cut the remaining cheese in half   They were there all night it got stuffy   But there will always be   if we go on cutting it in half   the cheese   ⁕

*_The Indian_ stands for all of us as in "the plight of the Indian"
**_Native American_ is not singular not specific   it must qualify
*** _Native AmericanS_ are a collective   a meaningful use of an umbrella term
****fewer _Native AmericanS_ live on reservations than live elsewhere
*****estimates of dollars spent on persistent social problems makes one wish they just paid cash
******Grandparents raise a significant percentage of Native youth   this has always been so
*******Certificate (Degree) of Indian Blood both heritage and pedigree (a paper we all know)
********Federal government recognizes at least 1/4 degree Indian blood _from one tribe_ no less
*********Federal recognition requires certified 1/4 degree Indian blood (don't bleed)
**********Some tribes have done away with the blood quantum requirement
***********Commodity foods are a cheap way Feds meet treaty obligations
************Minnesotans can be oppressively polite (Minnesota Nice) and racially despairing

The Bully Treaty

Expectations = champagne left popping in the flute
Excused myself from the room   the house
                                    head in hands on the stoop
while a phrase loops   *this is how it breaks*
                            this is how it breaks
                            this is how it breaks

            Stunned media   mistaken polls

still somehow my hands   just meat in my lap say
                        you knew   *it had to break*
            before it all could be fixed

Too gut sick to drink then   or look at white men   chuffed
on a plane the next day

Broken   as a treaty
the one between us   and them
                                    that meant civility

A great curtain drew aside
everyone else could see   what we always knew

what used to scurry against the light
Cousin Misogynist   Uncle Gun Nut   Granny Xenophobe

Then the gloating grin   that one I know
Boys   will be boys   will be justice   victim too
                    too heavy to push off us
                    just horsing around   just a joke

like the meme reads

        NOT STOLEN—CONQUERED

      across a map of the U.S.A.

which also names a dozen battles   *massacres defeats genocides*

red dots across the shapes of states   *homelands nations territories*

So simple   they want things simple

They are the same   they   who take now took then

the same that used to

        grab me   smirk at my body

        tell me   *shut up your smart mouth*

                who's so smart now?

What meme would it take to tell them? Tell their grandsons?

No fair fight ever fought at a single one of those dots

           massacres defeats genocides

How impossible my life has been

teaching student after student again and again

Even my *smart mouth* bends when it reads

any treaty   irreducible to meme

I could write NOT STOLEN—SWINDLED   across that map

and draw borders back   *homelands nations territories* to shapes of lakes and rivers

        and the names the land retains in our tongues

           expand that to our many nations' borders

See how it all balloons and enlarges?

           It's getting big now really too big

              like a complex thought

Territory 73 Mph

This is a complexity   the BIA   the DNR   no one can explain to me
right-of-way
territory   reduced by lines on a highway   ceded lands
           they took   I take
           photos so I can relate   to place

blue galaxy   my eye in my hand   protected   otter-skinned box
my precious   perceptive of   *field-reed-road-rise-fire in weeds*

controlled burn   grubbed out windbreak   living fence
                red willow—dogwood—kinnikinnick

at 73 mph
it is all ours
        again
                ancestors always present in the past
a few grandfathers back   dog sled mail carrier along this track

I-94
east or west
ottertail county   wildlife in windbreaks   highway right-of-way

way home way back way to know the world   as a girl
window cranked   world spun out   circles back
same as train tricks the eye   you fly   land stands still

Hwy 210
wahpeton to fergus falls
           creature-mapped   birds of previous years
           muskrat—kit fox-   *eagle -wheat ears-*

what happened to the wheat ears   those dapper swirls at road's edge?
they were here just a year ago for fifty years   fifty winters
whirl by   cell eye stills   captures   grass silver glass contrast

                                        fallow fold furrow
                                        black blue white

way home way back way to know the world   at 73 mph

highest resolution   point and tap   magic in that

app tags the image *dalton*   tags *battle lake*

who battled there?   ancestors always present in the past

pressed pillager band   pressed dakota

we've been again defied   defiled by a march   power towers concern the DNR

                    HELICOPTERS AT WORK   DO NOT LOOK UP

            FLASHES AND LOUD BOOMS POSSIBLE   DO NOT STOP

impossible not to gawk

great river energy   ottertail power
                    swans on nest—wheel of pelicans—little green heron

wind in towers   wind power   we all wanted wind
wanted transit but not trains   wanted wind but not towers
metal faintly reflective glare-proofed to vague gray   now

lavender hand holding monsters   miles and miles and miles
lines violent against a sky we thought was ours
                                  what we had left of ours

my hand-eye weapon   blind aim   I take you
take you back   way back   way home
                                                right-of-way

Mod World

Over the wax tacky still   or bluing sweet as violet
                            ammonia of cleanliness
whirling in checked skirt
        until my head hurts and I fall   the fakey fall of
                    we all fall down
Flat on the boards on the vinyl on the crush of plastic rock
        granite patterned formica table
        all the faux woods of a mod world
        Under table view
a clock sparked full of turquoise arms
            neighbor ladies   cigarettes and a crystal ashtray
      they call for me
                but won't work me out of my hiding
Time meant nothing yet
just a spiked metal disk clicking numbers   pointing all over the blue-green
                            neighbor kitchen
Chippewa ladies laughs crack higher and higher
              their lives a mess   they say
        less mess than
        dark rings of water   stray marks   all the residue
             they complain of
      You won't work it out   they say
            you won't work it out at all

The World Rotates

1.

We were so many so girl boy boy girl boy girl girl and cousins more and uncles more and aunties more and neighbors more and we were all

                         all the same in our world of the Indian School

Red brick steps and waxed floors and ladies laughing   all the babies and the moms their high hair in nets and deep shine of blue black waves curled and set and red lips made up to float over maternity smocks gingham peach pale blue a hundred buttons tiny rows and rows of shells

                  Every mom smelled clean   smoky   spray starched

Moms picked us up and set us down at random

                  Dads melted into the scene   picked us up   swung us round

See the world rotate

                      see the world from up there at a man's arms-length

                                    almost see how they

                                        see the world

2.

Next world   town world   mail slot doorbell lantern lights sliding closet doors long curtains
glass doors white woodwork   and gold leaf high-low retractable (doomed) bubble light
kitchen glow of copper handles fancy pendant fixtures rosy wood stainless dishwasher
lazy susan sprayer handle double sink

                    I wondered how our old kitchen could fit in all of it
or if I'd find our old bedroom upstairs
Everyone across the street seemed gray and old and bent so far down I thought
                                        they would all be kind
When the postman came I hid   a nice white-headed man but full of questions
                    Mom quietly shut shut shut the door   too slow
Somewhere else began   and began our forgetting the world   a world ago

Peacemaking

We long ago made a peace   a treaty
between enemy neighbors
like this
striped blankets   sashes worked with colored beads   animal-shaped pipes
of red stone   iron hatchets inlaid with lead designs   flutes carved to look
like a duck or goose   belts woven with colored threads   brass bells
copper water vessels   red wool   rich gifts to seal the peace

Sometimes the deal did not go down

Some wanted more   to be upheld as great men   (yes   only men)

We take your names with us to speak in honor of your greatness always
and when we ever hear your name, we will say "That is a great man you speak of"
and we will tell the stories of all the deeds you've done and how fine a figure you
made, how arrayed in fine clothes, and how many horses and how large your voice . . .

You get the idea

Except we had to mean it   *irreversibly*
Even though those men might have stolen   broken families   murdered
or maybe it was their thieving sons we killed   even then we had to forget
and mean what we said

Imagine how hard it would be to humble ourselves to humanity
Tell their stories as if they were our brothers-fathers-kinfolk — with pride
As if just making peace with them made them relatives whose shine
shined on us

We seek your peace now
for futures we cannot gift amends
unless like this

sleep   under blankets   beads of bright creatures pollinating flowers   animals
red as stone   or iron   flute song   duck and goose
                                                                earth full of microbes
and minerals   sun stored to serve you   wind making light and nights cool enough
water and vessels to drink   all once a given   then a gift   future riches

You get the idea
We came in peace but   left the aftermath of war like mud tracked in
messed up your carpets and ate all your bread
left milk jugs empty in the fridge and worse   much worse

Let our peace be one you can reverse
No gift can be enough   if we left you and
even gone   we keep stealing your summers   leaving just the storms
if we left you winters brutal beyond history   birds gone and bugs in tornadoes
all the fish gutted   water run off

It would be OK then   to reverse the peace we made when you were born
You do not need to hold up our names   *irreversibly*
only do not curse as you say them or
please   leave us off as relatives
make us ancestors only   as worthy as names on paper   signs

                                        Uphold the great ones
                                                and if we can't be them
                                        don't speak our names at all

No Use

When my bear nature comes upon me after snow arrival I sink into the blackness into the dark curve of sleep then a cave seeps behind my eyes (dark punctuation surrounds me) Oh let me be ease myself let me lumber and slumber off the fat of me forget the year of human work I won't be woke no use to try my earth blanket pulled around me eyes shut as commas Oh leave me a nation of one and the cubs who barely wake me when they come my one use they suck me thin all winter No use to try to rouse me it takes a brace of hounds and gloved hands hauling me out by my legs No use no fight in me sleep stays on me like a drug If I form one thought it is for the cubs but I'm no use pulled free of earth unable to move unmoved until the last thought comes

I am the use
of their guns

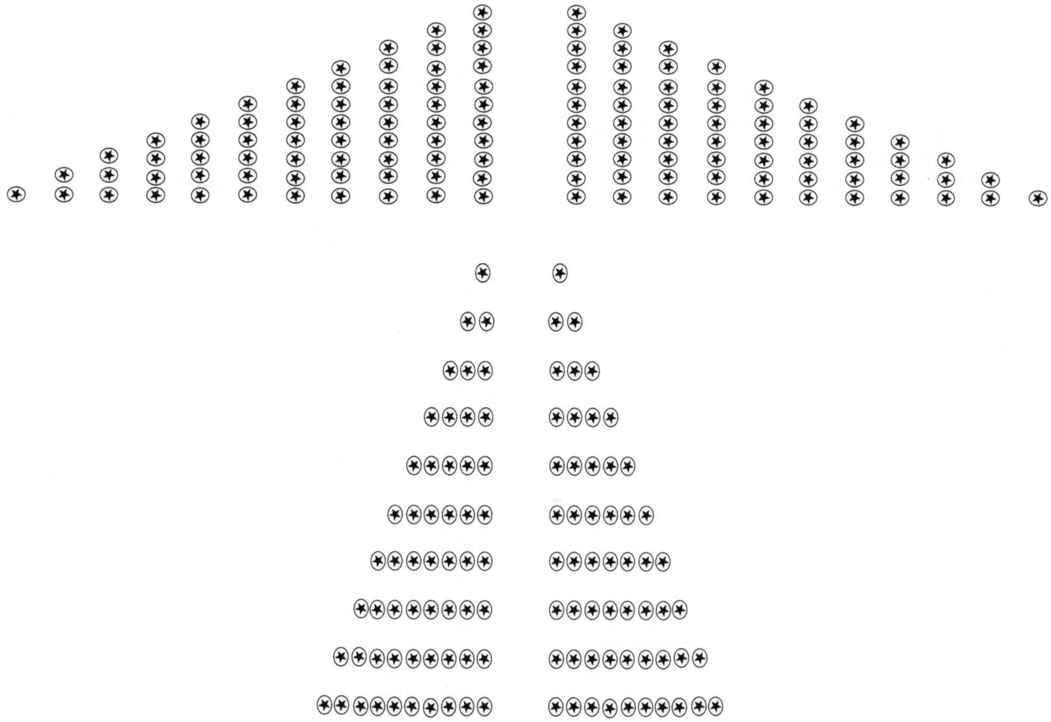

I Feel Like a Fool Do You?

A tarot deck fool
looking back to see
if you are looking back at me
I'll trip right off that cliff

Once in North Dakota in my actual childhood I saw a hobo (that's what we said then)
with an actual red bandana bundle he had slung on a stick

He tried to get me to walk under a bridge with him   he said he had *a great gift*
my bigger sister sniggered at that   or there'd be
                                        a red dress hanging in a tree for me too

Which brings me back to that fool
tumbling ass over tea kettle
into some gully
having fallen for it

then dusting fool self's ass off
pick yourself up   start all over again

This is a world of men
this tarot deck and sure   *The World*
and yet I won't give a single pronoun for it

We were both fools
we are all fools

Once in my actual adult life   in a hideous time of lies
                                our own stories were required of us

Fool though I feel   real and truly fucked though we be   I picked

                                    my first person

I set my truth free

                                fool   me fool   me fool me

Aftermath

1 = hurt before I had the words   I'd take the blame in confession   at age seven

2 = next on a slide   I kicked that big boy and ran   he laughed   surprised I'd fight

Time turned me past all excuse of childish acts

3–30 = their hands   grab poke snatch grope probe   backed me into lockers or hallways or
        fences or trees   (not counting) their threats   gangs bricks knives fists

31 = babysitting   the dad's buddy snuck back from the bar   chased me around the kitchen
        like the big bad wolf in a cartoon   too drunk he huffed and puffed   fell down

32 = "the first"   I said no   that should have been enough   he pushed
        said   just give it up   and I asked what   what should I give up?   while I did

33 = how many times that voice inside said "get it over with—don't get hurt"   so I endured

We unknew our own word no

34 = drunk boyfriend got on top   woke me up   I shoved him out then off the bed
        I said no then   "bad dog" he laughed from the floor   I slept   the end

35 = the cop who drove me home   I told him no don't start   he stopped in the fog
        to let me know exactly what he could do   before I'd be dead   if he wanted to
        all he meant was   for me to know   for my own good   he said
        I stared at the mirror   the pine tree   red and scented   dangling there
                                                                              the reek so cherry sweet

I never thought I'd gotten the worst   I never meant to calculate my hurts or keep score   I can barely remember all that happened by half

                              until it all adds up   our bodies do that math

The Other Night

The house phone rang and you weren't home

Quick turned off the light and looked into the street—
      street bright with light snow and no tracks up the step

I picked it up *Just a minute*—ice still in my glass I clinked
      for background noise and to no one *Honey*   *I'm on the phone—*
      OK   *sorry*   *hi?*

No one there meant someone maybe there meant
                       my right to my lies

Nonfiction Craft Lesson in March

It is not wrong to speak it—who you were when young who you wish to be when old　　It is not wrong to speak of the ones who moved you who moved through you　　It is only that it is hard

A little hard　　It leaves a mild mineral tang

We have always known our view is skewed by place culture sex gender and the order of your coming into being among a tumble of siblings　　cousins too　　All of this made you—made the you who sees who focuses the lens who focuses on those you wish to speak of　　those you wish to relate Or not wish　　but sometimes must　　relate　　And if those we must speak of will read our words? Or live with what others read?

Shall we speak only of the dead?

That seems less right at times　　to speak of the dead　　I do not mean the defenseless dead or the revered dead of long ago　　I mean the dead who withdrew their names from our mouths

We do not speak of them

We do not speak to them so they do not answer　　We do not speak those names *in order* that they not answer　　We no longer want to hear their voices　　and though they sometimes mutter　it matters that they are not bid to speak

Maple sap runs clear although the hardwood heart of maple is almost red　　Maple darkens as it distills　boils down　　condenses and sugars　A leaf of cedar minds the boil　　Make whatever metaphor you will　　I am simply reminded of maple when I think of the dead

The Coldness Was Coldness

1.
This is just to say

I have eaten the plums
Etc
Etc
Icebox
Etc
Etc

With the exception that the plums were not plums and the sweetness was not sweetness and that I did not eat them but instead carried them next door to tempt the sad woman I sometimes see smoking on the flagstones

2.
Wm Carlos Wms was a Doctor and husband of Mrs Dr Wm Carlos Wms who has remained nameless to me faceless to me except for a frown and dark brows on a pale forehead What I have learned about _____Williams is that she could swim and had been an Atlantic Certified Life-guard considered herself one of the early gourmets in the U.S. and was often a guest of Mrs Julia Child   Mrs Dr Wms suffered from what we might now call depression what we might now call ennui what we might now call boredom what we might now call god-awful stultification Etc Etc I say this but it is just to say a fiction

3.
This is not to say

I wouldn't have eaten the plums
Etc
Etc
But no matter how cold or sweet
Etc
Etc
I would not have eaten them alone

Red Language

If I heard the words you once used
in our wild place rough with scrub roses
in sand —If your words came back
gray and kind as mild winter
believe me I'd still understand
offer my own red language
my tongue to your tongue
so we recall what we once said
that made us live
                    made us choose to live

Wild Turkey

Not the bottle
Not the burn on the lips
lit throat glow
Not even wild   really
but a small-town bird
whose burgundy throat
shimmers like nothing ever
A huge bird   impressive
who lurches and stalks me
window to window in this
desert retreat
What does he want?
Clearly he is lonely
pecks his reflection
and speaks to it in a low *gubble*
(not gobble) gubbles so tenderly
Soon as I think of him   his eye hits on me
We have watched each other for days
His shifting colors fascinate me his territorial strut
But it is his bald and blue-red head
his old man habits and gait that move me
If I even think of him   I taste whiskey
Drunk on solitude   I'd talk to anybody
I try his language on my lips
His keen response burns like shame

Stone Animate

Whether creation carved them or not
my hands are some concretion
some tawn of rock   washed over
and over in surf until sand encases the glow
of quartz   hardness thrust up through earth's crust
to tumble a hundred million years
and here we reach each other
I reach out with hands that match this skipping stone
and I think a moment   we know each other   and though
for the purposes of art I should   I will not let you go

We Singular

Make us lichen   make
my body our body
                   a colony eating air and light   each other
       making god
with our exchange of DNA and coded info

we would be entire   enveloping   beyond boundaries

     we'd make art outlining branches
                     even pinecones
just because we could   we body

would be but no   just my body sole   solitary   alone
      trying to sense   impossible task
       millions of teeming others

lives of cells   virus germ   creatures swimming in my tears
healers harmers
everyone artless and automatic

      should feel like love   union reunion
      should feel like   creation
                should

How It Escaped Our Attention

When a whole being
births into your hands
still you see your hands
no matter how unworldly
the beauty of the child

Then the universe of words
works past cosmology
to a useful name   a handle
in English unlike the Indigenous
genderless language of verbs

Moon blues   comet misses
moon looms super   moon bleeds
many cosmological shifts later
our hands eclipsed by
the lovely being come so far

Come closer than ever
across the several heavens
we Ojibwe name
the layers of our atmosphere
and further out there
the fourth sky   forever sky

When you first came to us
we did not have an Ojibwe name
to know the sky beyond
the sky beyond the sky

How were we to know
he was she was
they are
you

How were we to know who?

The Eighth Fire

Deepest skies   when finally we arrive   dark as fire mark on rock
no scorched scent   but cold as when   we prod the ash
     we wish for coals

Dark into which swirls the million stars obscured these many years—
spiral knowledge unfurls or funnels us while white rocks reveal
     years before the years before the years

We speak in verbs   active as water   dark water the well of what we know
what we always knew

     talk water's talk
     unseen we walk   a dark path
     carried along on a spiral
     we go forward
     when we're back

Oh—Terrible Movie!

Slogging on snowshoes 40 urban miles
Ice crevasse replaced by glass roof of a mall
        Manhattan's the destination   of course
terrible movies require a ruined NYC circa 2007
            a climate collapse at least telegraphed
art direction's not bad
Lady Liberty iced over   hair blown into icicles a hundred feet long
Simpatico audience   in this Polar Vortex   2019
we huddle in a house blazed to 60F   not bad   but drafts dance cobwebs
        frosted windows ping   the whole house groans
we groan too   Oh—Terrible Movie!
             How we love thee
disaster flicks   train our kids   to win the apocalypse
so proud when the kid knows the heroes got it wrong
He doesn't even have on gloves!   *Use food to distract the wolves!*
odd intimacy when we holler OH NO
        because the refuge turns out to be   THE LIBRARY
        librarians portrayed as passive and nerdy   Who are they?
        librarians we know   could find the Holy Grail
            shelved in Mysteries somewhere
        or at least know how to research   R-values of newsprint
        corn chip fuel or hand sanitizer fire starters

Never mind   I'm already proud   as soon as she sees the stacks
our kid yells   outraged   *Let me guess*
        THEY BURN THE BOOKS (she never would)
            but   Reader
                they do

When Mega Fungi Roamed the Earth

How blooming   how immense   how they towered
multicolored and florescent   obscene or umbrellas or wings
phenomenal funk of wetness or overwhelming warmth of butter or honey

None yet grazed upon they   they collected   they networked   slo-mo
tendrils of mycelium   lightning in black loam   prickling circuits
formed   an intelligence   an influence
dreamed into the height of night branches   our mammal ancestors
then withdrew when they witnessed   or visioned
                what would become
                      of us

~

Mega Fungi move
      in infinite   slowness
we hardly   notice

~

they were gods
gone underground   speaking through tree rot
root grown and grotesque   over time they
                fool us they
                  feed us they

                  feed upon us

If I Give You a Last Lesson

If we had just these moments   I would tell you
Stand close as I write
Hold my shoulders   last touch
                                                 then I'll be gone

How to watch me go   how my being will dwindle   all twilight
How to stand here alone when I am gone   feel the vibrant earth rotate through you
                                                 until your head accepts
How to listen for what's left of me   my voice that jolts you out of weekend sleep
          that wonders what you eat   asks you to demand real love
                                             from anyone you give your sweetest self
How to take into yourself all the structures I pointed out   the physical logic   my rationale
          the critical angle you can use so quickly your wit can outrace your body
                                             and give you that moment to jump
How to jump when an enemy
How to know which branch   which roof   which window
How to yearn for blue shores   moments alone   when you know
                                                            all you will know
                                  and can read it back to yourself
How to relearn   what you don't know
How to dive   hold your breath so bubbles fill the water popping
                          full of reflections of your own face
                          and you are not afraid
How to not be afraid you can say it

                          I am not afraid to learn

How to live with the hurt of being human
                          How you learn it is you say   *it hurts*
How in itself it is the lesson

                          How you say *gone now*   and *still here*

Now watch me go   my being will dwindle all twilight
and other words that combine *w* with another consonant unexpectedly

That last to make you laugh
                              last lesson you live all your life
so when you go you pass it on

Dream of the Land-Based Future

Service took the place of romance
in the land-based future that I dreamt as past
There on grassy bluffs above great marshes   rivers   prairies
            we felt related to hawks most of all
                we made hawk indulgences   metaphors
If we believed in anything we could not see   we held dear
the return of hawks   hawks meant mice   mice meant herds

A man's seriousness   his falcon-like summary of what he saw   engaged me deeply
Love we allowed   as long as we remained the hands of the earth
as long as every movement was for earth   and our work
so if our love did not matter to a future   we refrained
refraining held its own energy   power of inertia   it burned

Side by side for years we gazed and never touched   it wasn't hard
my yearning I gave over to something greater
it enlarged then and made me shy
to look on his long fingers his brown neck his ruff of stubble his stained shirt and long thighs
At times we'd match our eyes we'd pause to nod   acknowledge love
so it fueled work so hard to do   so needed beyond us somewhere

No one told us   do this   we all agreed   without rules
we were the kind who survived to live those times

We opened dams   long-before dismantled every human structure   save one
We planned for the sake of land returning   we surveyed daily
we worked it with our ideas and gathered most minute understandings to mull
we were religious but not god-minded   in retreat to seek more perfect understanding
We stood on overlooks and awaited changes in the water grass bluffs
we awaited the animals   yearned for them most of all
there were no songbirds   hawks were hope of herds

Hawk-named drones we used in our constant survey

When at last we learned   herds were headed our way
                                            we planned a kind of Holy Day
We maintained one human place   a huge arena where we spoke as a group
as those who thought   not leaders   just reporters   information sources
we worked in groups to produce our words as solemn or raucous as poems but not art
we never spoke of it as anything but science   and were humbled when
our words elated everyone assembled   each year

We prepared for the crowd to come to see the herds pass
teams made of sisters arrived to clean and we cleaned with them
the patterns and rhythms we made we projected   a drone's view to share
so beautiful and so pleasing   ecstatic moment we fell into
                                            synchronous and fluid

Into my work flashed another yearning   for a sister a   mother a   someone woman
who might let me speak of the man and love   who let me lean to her
I could see her dark hair and serious kind face   she felt warm next to me   most dear
She and the man   his scent and her sensation   I would not keep
these I gave to the dust cloth   the thousand rusted seats
                                            the thunder of the world to come

Reprieve

We did not expect the light to break
                                   into prism and the earth to cool

A new deluge—knowledge   we waded
                                                         praised
so much we did not know we did not know

                                   We missed
the purple of snow shadow—but kept snow   Snow!

Our skins struggled into iridescence
                                   everyone grew new
                                   we knew not
who walked among us

Locks dropped off   some felt a loss
                         clocks stopped   they
                                                   shut up days
walked out nights

                         Some gave up when Jesus did not come

fine we thought   we're done with dying

                         Now this   this shimmer
                         everlasting lake of time
            when every child born is ours   every child mine

AUTHOR'S NOTES

The cover art by Andrea Carlson is from her 2019 print *Exit*, which she describes as a "sigil for warding off loss." Her statement on the image follows my own brief contextual notes below.

During the Polar Vortex of 2019, I did not leave my drafty house in Minnesota for five solid days. Many of these poems were written or revised during that deeply cold period when schools were closed, meetings canceled, and everyone hunkered down to binge watch and scroll, wonder, and worry about us all. This collection begins with a question, goes on to consider answers, and tries to understand the mechanics of abuse. Maybe if we understand it we can stop it?

Although I've crafted these poems for various audiences, both Native/ Ojibwe and others, some bits of information might add a layer of intimacy and understanding, so I offer the following:

"How" uses the phrase "wintry mix" which is now a more frequent slushy weather condition in Minnesota due to climate change. "Parhelion" and "paraselene," known as sun dogs and moon dogs, are brilliant and otherworldly rings and orbs that appear near the sun and moon in sub-zero temperatures.

"Variations True" references the German town Pforzheim, which was firebombed in World War II, killing my great-grandparents. A non-military target that included injured Allied troops, the city was reduced to rubble. Many of my relatives survived, and I met them there in 1979.

"All Nations" refers to the fall 2019 news that the wild bird population has declined by nearly one-third in the past fifty years. You can read more at birds.cornell.edu/home/bring-birds-back. This poem also mentions 1950's Termination policy, or House Concurrent Resolution 108, meant to end federal treaty obligations to tribes and to withdraw legal protection of Native Nations' rights to land, culture, and religion.

"Fauxskins" refers to the page "List of writers from people of indigenous to the Americas" on Wikipedia. For better insight, you might read Wikipedia pages on "passing: Passing as Indigenous Americans," as well as "Native American identity in the United States."

"Not" is not about any one girl who grew up in a small, mostly white town on the plains.

"Story of the Charismenace" is a fanciful retelling of an internet staple, those oft-circulating listicles usually titled something like "10 Ways to Stop an Abusive Narcissist." #1 = Disengage.

"Territory Was Not Virgin and Neither Was I (Virgin)" refers to weapons used on unarmed humans at Standing Rock on the night of November 20, 2016. Friends camped there texted me unforgettable live video. Police later admitted to using stinger rounds and teargas grenades banned by many U.S. law enforcement agencies, pepper spray, Mace, Tasers, and a sound weapon. The sound weapon causes haunting flashbacks.

"North of Love" is a poem about, among other things, people who are being stalked and surveilled who take a walk on a frozen lake even though they are visible for miles around.

The website "BearAncestry.com" does not exist and there is no genetic test for your clan animal.

"Melania Won't Leave You (though she retires to her private island Melanesia where she learns the Tongan word *tabu*)" is informed by the definition of "tabu" (or taboo), which comes from a Tongan word and translates as "to be set apart," according to www.oxfordreference.com.

"Big Sir" contains a reference to Vantablack, an engineered black, often referred to as "blackest black," that absorbs almost all light. The color is owned by Surrey NanoSystems.

"Little Big" and the collection title, *Little Big Bully*, are meant as passing echoes of the book *Little Big Man* by Thomas Berger and the film directed by Arthur Penn. I am interested in how some Indigenous names successfully hold contradictions that, when translated into English, seem unresolved.

"Zeno's Indians" refers to numerous statistics about Native American lives. The best source for these is the website for National Congress of American Indians, www.ncai.org/about-tribes/demographics.

"The Bully Treaty." I use treaty-making as metaphor. To better understand treaties, see *The Relentless Business of Treaties* by Martin Case (St. Paul, MN: Minnesota Historical Society Press, 2018).

"Territory 73 Mph" refers to the Department of Natural Resources, DNR. It might help to know that erecting high-voltage power lines along interstates involves complex land ownership and environmental issues. Many people lose their land to eminent domain and tribes are rarely consulted. This poem shares some of the obsessions about highways in Andrea Carlson's art.

"Peacemaking" refers to accounts of the 1870 treaty between the Dakota and Ojibwe signed at Fort Abercrombie in North Dakota. Our great-grandfather was there serving as an altar boy to the negotiating priest.

"No Use" considers current attempts to make legal killing bears and cubs as they hibernate.

"I Feel Like a Fool Do You?" mentions a red dress, which is the emblem for Missing and Murdered Indigenous Women, https://www.csvanw.org/mmiw/.

"The Coldness Was Coldness" responds to William Carlos Williams's poem "This Is Just To Say."

"Wild Turkey" is a Marfa poem.

"We Singular" responds to a talk by Robin Wall Kimmerer, author of *Braiding Sweetgrass*.

"How It Escaped Our Attention" references the lack of gender pronouns in Ojibwe language.

"Oh! Terrible Movie!": the film referred to is *The Day After Tomorrow*.

"Reprieve" is based on the supposition that there are colors we cannot see, and that if something dramatic happened to our atmosphere we could see differently, or we should.

COVER ARTIST'S NOTE | Andrea Carlson

Based on one's vantage point or cultural expectations, the significance of a place can become lost. The West as a colonial project produced descriptions of the "Americas" as new land, a new world, while actively destroying and uprooting evidence of ancient history. One example of this can be seen in the defacement of ancient effigy mounds throughout Wisconsin. Hundreds of massive, shallow mounds depicting birds, lizards, men, panthers, and snakes blanket the landscape. Many of the ancient mounds have been destroyed, dissected by roads, or they were flattened by settler farmers who couldn't or wouldn't see the mounds for what they were.

Exit is a print about absence and propagating presence. A potential exit can represent a fear. Within Indigenous communities exists a deep-seated fear of losing cultural practices, languages, and art forms. With this in mind, *Exit* is also a print about that fear. Specifically, the print references ancient Indigenous creations (Man Mound of Baraboo, Wisconsin, mica hand/talon forms of the Mississippian peoples) that have been falsely attributed to non-natives, lost tribes, and extinct peoples.

The imagery within this print signifies conflicting directions and a state of exposure. Bent tree trail markers, created by tethering saplings to the ground to produce bent grown trees used as directional markers. These trees are found all over North America, are publicly accessible, and vulnerable to destruction. Disembodied hands signing "exit" or "outside" in American Sign Language emerge from these trees, flanked by a bird stone. Images of overlapping mica cutouts of hands and talons hover at the center.

Because prints are editioned and produced in multiple they have the ability to make a single image diasporic. This inherent quality of the print is my sigil for warding off loss. The imagery of this print represents an attempt at reparative presence for the space between the Twin Cities and

Chicago, the lands of several Anishinaabe tribes, Dakota and Ho-Chunk people. This print is meant to be a sigil for the thought forms of those who travel I-94, the road that cuts through mound country. To those who have seen this print and travel I-94, perhaps their minds will contemplate the profound significance of that space.

PHOTO BY CHRIS FELVER

HEID E. ERDRICH is the author of seven collections of poetry. Her writing has won fellowships and awards from Native Arts and Cultures Foundation, McKnight Foundation, Minnesota State Arts Board, Bush Foundation, Loft Literary Center, and First People's Fund, and she has twice won a Minnesota Book Award for poetry. She was also the editor of the 2018 anthology *New Poets of Native Nations*, which was the recipient of an American Book Award from the Before Columbus Foundation and a Midwest Booksellers Choice Award. Erdrich works as a visual arts curator and collaborator, and as an educator. She teaches in the low-residency MFA Creative Writing Program of Augsburg University and is the 2019–2020 Distinguished Visiting Professor in Liberal Arts at the University of Minnesota Morris. Erdrich grew up in Wahpeton, North Dakota, and is Ojibwe enrolled at Turtle Mountain. She lives in Minnesota.

GAROUS ABDOLMALEKIAN
Lean Against This Late Hour

PAIGE ACKERSON-KIELY
Dolefully, A Rampart Stands

JOHN ASHBERY
Selected Poems
Self-Portrait in a
  Convex Mirror

PAUL BEATTY
Joker, Joker, Deuce

JOSHUA BENNETT
Owed
The Sobbing School

TED BERRIGAN
The Sonnets

LAUREN BERRY
The Lifting Dress

JOE BONOMO
Installations

PHILIP BOOTH
Lifelines: Selected Poems
  1950–1999
Selves

JIM CARROLL
Fear of Dreaming: The
  Selected Poems
Living at the Movies
Void of Course

ALISON HAWTHORNE
DEMING
Genius Loci
Rope
Stairway to Heaven

CARL DENNIS
Another Reason
Callings
New and Selected Poems
  1974–2004
Night School
Practical Gods
Ranking the Wishes
Unknown Friends

DIANE DI PRIMA
Loba

STUART DISCHELL
Backwards Days
Dig Safe

STEPHEN DOBYNS
Velocities: New and
  Selected Poems:
  1966–1992

EDWARD DORN
Way More West

HEID E. ERDRICH
Little Big Bully

ROGER FANNING
The Middle Ages

ADAM FOULDS
The Broken Word: An Epic
  Poem of the British Empire
  in Kenya, and the Mau Mau
  Uprising Against It

CARRIE FOUNTAIN
Burn Lake
Instant Winner

AMY GERSTLER
Dearest Creature
Ghost Girl
Medicine
Nerve Storm
Scattered at Sea

EUGENE GLORIA
Drivers at the Short-Time
  Motel
Hoodlum Birds
My Favorite Warlord
Sightseer in This Killing City

DEBORA GREGER
By Herself
Desert Fathers, Uranium
  Daughters
God
In Darwin's Room
Men, Women, and Ghosts
Western Art

TERRANCE HAYES
American Sonnets for My Past
  and Future Assassin
Hip Logic
How to Be Drawn
Lighthead
Wind in a Box

NATHAN HOKS
The Narrow Circle

ROBERT HUNTER
Sentinel and Other Poems

MARY KARR
Viper Rum

WILLIAM KECKLER
Sanskrit of the Body

JACK KEROUAC
Book of Blues
Book of Haikus
Book of Sketches

JOANNA KLINK
Circadian
Excerpts from a Secret
  Prophecy
The Nightfields
Raptus

JOANNE KYGER
As Ever: Selected Poems

ANN LAUTERBACH
Hum
If in Time: Selected Poems,
  1975–2000
On a Stair
Or to Begin Again
Spell
Under the Sign

CORINNE LEE
Plenty
Pyx

PHILLIS LEVIN
May Day
Mercury
Mr. Memory & Other Poems

PATRICIA LOCKWOOD
Motherland Fatherland
  Homelandsexuals

WILLIAM LOGAN
Macbeth in Venice
Madame X
Rift of Light
Strange Flesh
The Whispering Gallery

J. MICHAEL MARTINEZ
Museum of the Americas

ADRIAN MATEJKA
The Big Smoke
Map to the Stars
Mixology

MICHAEL MCCLURE
Huge Dreams: San Francisco
  and Beat Poems

ROSE MCLARNEY
Forage
Its Day Being Gone

DAVID MELTZER
David's Copy: The Selected
  Poems of David Meltzer

ROBERT MORGAN
Dark Energy
Terroir

CAROL MUSKE-DUKES
Blue Rose
An Octave Above Thunder:
  New and Selected Poems
Red Trousseau
Twin Cities

ALICE NOTLEY
Certain Magical Acts
Culture of One
The Descent of Alette
Disobedience
For the Ride
In the Pines
Mysteries of Small Houses

WILLIE PERDOMO
The Crazy Bunch
The Essential Hits of Shorty
  Bon Bon

DANIEL POPPICK
Fear of Description

LIA PURPURA
It Shouldn't Have Been
  Beautiful

LAWRENCE RAAB
The History of Forgetting
Visible Signs: New and
  Selected Poems

BARBARA RAS
The Last Skin
One Hidden Stuff

MICHAEL ROBBINS
Alien vs. Predator
The Second Sex

PATTIANN ROGERS
Generations
Holy Heathen Rhapsody
Quickening Fields
Wayfare

SAM SAX
Madness

ROBYN SCHIFF
A Woman of Property

WILLIAM STOBB
Absentia
Nervous Systems

TRYFON TOLIDES
An Almost Pure Empty
  Walking

VINCENT TORO
Tertulia

SARAH VAP
Viability

ANNE WALDMAN
Gossamurmur
Kill or Cure
Manatee/Humanity
Trickster Feminism

JAMES WELCH
Riding the Earthboy 40

PHILIP WHALEN
Overtime: Selected Poems

ROBERT WRIGLEY
Anatomy of Melancholy and
  Other Poems
Beautiful Country
Box
Earthly Meditations: New and
  Selected Poems
Lives of the Animals
Reign of Snakes

MARK YAKICH
The Importance of Peeling
  Potatoes in Ukraine
Spiritual Exercises
Unrelated Individuals
  Forming a Group Waiting
  to Cross